Romantic SOUTH DEVON COAST

LEE PENGELLY

HALSGROVE

First published in Great Britain in 2009

British Library Cataloguing-in-Publication Data
A CIP record for this title is available from the British Library

ISBN 978 1 84114 858 8

HALSGROVE
Halsgrove House,
Ryelands Industrial Estate,
Bagley Road, Wellington, Somerset TA21 9PZ
Tel: 01823 653777   Fax: 01823 216796
email: sales@halsgrove.com

Part of the Halsgrove group of companies
Information on all Halsgrove titles is available at: www.halsgrove.com

Printed and bound by Grafiche Flaminia, Italy

For Abi & Zak – the lights of my life

ACKNOWLEDGEMENTS

I would like to thank the following for help in producing this book:

Jan Barwick & Jane Fitzgerald – Devon Life
Spectrum Photo Labs – Plymouth
Tourist Information – Plymouth
My Wife – for her patience when the lights good

INTRODUCTION

I am a landscape photographer at heart and love nothing more than photographing the great outdoors. I favour many types of landscape from rolling countryside to wild rugged moorland but to be honest I am happiest out on the coast with the waves lapping around my feet.

I am fortunate to live within easy reach of great coastal locations in every direction, all within a short drive, or even a walk if I am feeling fit. There is something about the coast that attracts me time and again, the motion of the waves, the ever changing tides and the sheer wilderness feeling, all combine to make the coastline a special place for me.

The coast is undeniably romantic, as the title of this book suggests, and I have tried to convey this with my selection of pictures. There are many 'romantic' locations along Devon's South Coast, some with intriguing tales of pirates and smugglers others just picturesque and beautiful. At each location I have immersed myself in the place and tried to capture the essence of it. Some places are very special to me, others such as Slapton, where my camera took an impromptu dip in the lake, I will always remember, but on the whole this book has given me the chance to record my favourite landscape for posterity.

This book has been compiled mainly from new work taken on my Nikon D2X digital SLR camera although there are a handful of older pictures from my files taken on trusty Fuji Velvia Slide film on various formats. My shooting style has changed over the years and to date my favourite technique is to capture motion, especially on the coast. Using long shutter speeds and Lee neutral density filters I create movement in waves enlivening the two-dimensional image. My camera equipment takes some knocks during it's working life no more so than out on the coast. Saltwater, sea spray and sand are all unsavoury things for a camera. My Nikon does have weatherproof seals but my gear needs constant maintenance. During the course of putting this book together I have lost a 18-70mm lens to the sea, walking boots to salt encrusting and a tripod to sand, but I can't resist returning again and again. More of my work can be found at *www.silverscenephoto.co.uk*.

Lee Pengelly, 2009

Weathered timber steps become part of the landscape on the narrow sand spit at Dawlish Warren.

Early morning sunlight on the sea defences at Dawlish Warren.

(Right) Waves turn to mist during a long exposure at dusk on Westcombe beach rocks.

Dusk over Westcombe bay.

Luxury yachts moored in Brixham Marina at dusk.

Brixham Harbour at dusk.

Last colour of the day reflecting in the wet sand at Westcombe.

After a stormy day the last light of the day under lights the brooding clouds over Westcombe bay beach.

Dusk over Plymouth Sound.

A long exposure smoothes the sea washing over the concrete jetty at Firestone bay.

Wildflower field behind Wembury church with views over the bay.

Last light over a stormy Wembury bay.

Dawn at Torquay.

The new swing bridge over Torquay harbour.

Rowing boats amongst the reeds at Slapton Ley

Torcross and Slapton Ley viewed from above at dawn.

Incoming tide washing around old wooden groynes at Teignmouth.

Teignmouth seafront at dusk.

In summer this busy jetty on Plymouth Sound, is in constant use by tourists boarding the 'Dockyard and Warships' tour boats. At dawn the place is tranquil and deserted.

Small trawler in Plymouth Sound, sunset.

Sand dunes and marram grasses on the edge of the Warren Reserve, Dawlish.

Colourful beach huts on Dawlish seafront.

Two walkers strolling along Mountbatten breakwater at dusk.

First light silhouettes luxury yachts at dawn in Sutton Harbour.

Dusk over the Mewstone at Wembury.

Waves washing out over the
beach at Wembury.

First light illuminates the old rickety fencing protecting the fragile sand dunes at Bantham, overlooking Bigury bay.

Dawn sunlight bursts though clouds illuminating the bay at Bigbury.

Wet sand reflects the dawn colour in the sky at Paignton beach.

Empty beach and red skies on a pre-dawn shoot at the pier on Paignton's seafront.

Moody red sunset over Thurlestone cove.

Yachts and fishing boats on still water at dawn near Kingsbridge.

Wooden groynes lead out on to an estuary view at dawn on the Exe river mouth.

Dawn on Exmouth Esplanade.

Dawn at Bovisand bay beach.

Waves washing into shore at Bovisand bay beach.

The West Devon Way footpath beside the picturesque tidal lake at Hooe.

Cottage ornée overlooking the beach at Sidmouth.

Deep sunset over the Tamar river at Warleigh Point.

A disused boat sits on the water's edge at dawn, with the Tamar bridges beyond.

Yachts and small boats moored on the Yealm at Newton Ferrers.

Last light over Westcombe bay.

Waves rush in over shoreline rocks at Hope Cove beach at sunset.

Dusk at Hope Cove.

Moored boats on the estuary at Salcombe
on a summer morning.

Looking across the estuary to Salcombe.

One lucky homeowner with a great view over the estuary at Mill Bay at Salcombe.

Waves rushing in around driftwood on the beach at Wembury.

Sea spray rolls in off the waves onto the idyllic beach at Blackpool Sands.

Blackpool Sands headland.

Atmospheric dawn at Castle Cove in Dartmouth.

Sailing dinghy on its way out to sea past the castle at Dartmouth.

A vivid sunset over the bay at Bovisand.

Misty sunrise over the Avon estuary.

Rough seas at Slapton Sands.

Cormorant drying
it's wings at dawn
on Slapton Ley.

Thatched boathouse at Bantham nestled in the landscape.

Looking across the dunes at Bantham towards Burgh Island.

The Mill Café overlooking Wembury beach on a stormy morning.

Warm dusk light over
Wembury bay.

Slapton Ley lake at Torcross.

Thatched cottage
at Torcross.

Jetty at Dawlish seafront.

Dawlish's very own Ayers Rock!

Rock-strewn cove on the coast at Wembury bay.

Summer morning on the Exeter canal at Turf Locks.

Brightly-coloured fishing trawlers in Torquay harbour.

Summer morning at Salcombe.

Salcombe viewed from Mill Bay.

The traditional pier at Torquay stretching around the harbour.

Last light of the day brings the sky to life over Thurlestone cove.

Wave wash at Thurlestone.

The last rays of the sun, Thurlestone.

Rocky shoreline at Hope cove.

Sunlight bursts through clouds over Hope Cove in winter.

The small town of Kingsbridge rising from an early summer mist.

Yacht and trawler moored on the glassy surfaced estuary, Kingsbridge.

Waves rushing in around foreshore boulder at Hallsands.

Dog walkers at low tide
on Goodrington beach.

Waves rushing out over an iron groyne buried in the sand on Teignmouths seafront.

Sunset illuminates the pier at
Teignmouth.

Barnacle-encrusted rock,
shaped lake a breaking wave.

Dawn sunrise at Ladram bay on the
East Devon coast.

The famous art deco hotel on Burgh Island is cut off from the mainland at high tide.

The famous island viewed through evening primroses.

First light on the rusting diving board on Plymouth's art deco seafront.

The ribs of the diving board seen against a dawn sky.

Vivid sunset over Wembury bay.

The setting sun turns rock pools red at the end of the day at Wembury Point.

A calm sea on the coast at Prawle Point.

Prawle Point. This headland is notoriously blustery and dangerous for shipping, but on a calm day it appears so serene.

Luxury yachts on the river at Salcombe

Salcombe.

Rich red cliffs at Orcombe

Sun bursts through heavy cloud over Orcombe seafront.

The quaint thatched boathouse at low tide, Bantham.

With each tide the beaches at Bigbury bay change, uncovering
large rocks, sand patterns and shells.

Sunrise over the beach at Exmouth.

Waves rushing in around seafront steps at Exmouth.

Fishing trawler working in Start Bay.

Atmospheric early dawn sunrise over the lighthouse at Start Point.

A frozen boardwalk leading through Dawlish Warren nature reserve.

First light on the marina at Starcross.

Storm clouds break, letting the sun's rays streak through momentarily over Start Bay.

Summer at Bayard's Cove
in Dartmouth.

Dawn sunlight backlights the pier on Paignton seafront.

The 'Hindoo' styled Redcliffe hotel overlooking the red sand beach on Paignton's seafront at dawn.

Steep banks of house overlooking Bayard's Cove in Dartmouth.

Dartmouth Castle overlooking Castle Cove at dawn.

Atmospheric sunset over Thurlestone Rock.

Waves rushing out over the beach at Thurlestone.

First light over Mothecombe beach.

Cliffs reflected in sand at dawn at Mothecombe beach.

A summer breeze through colourful plants on the headland overlooking the mouth of the River Yealm.

Tranquil water reflecting small boats on the River Yealm estuary.

The River Erme estuary snaking through the valley at Mothecombe.

First light on the Shag
Stone at Heybrook bay.

High tide at Hope Cove.

Spring tide flows in at sunset at Hope Cove.

Waves rushing in over the shingle beach at dawn at Ladram bay.

Gentle dawn light, Ladram bay.

Waves flow in around foreshore rocks on Stoke beach in the South Hams.

The enviably positioned holiday caravans at Stoke beach have a view to die for.

Shingle beach at Beesands.

(Left) Dawn light in Sutton Harbour, Plymouth.

Bright fishing trawlers moored at Plymouth's Barbican.

Synonymous with the British seaside but quaint all the same.

In need of a coat of paint but full of character!

The idyllic beach at Blackpool Sands on a summer morning.

Dawn on Blackpool Sands beach.

Little thatched boathouse on the Bantham estuary at low tide.

Colourful wildflowers on the cliff top overlooking Bantham beach in early summer.

Rich reedbed habitat on Slapton Ley.

Houses and reed beds at Torcross.

(Left) Incoming tide at Heybrook bay.

Early morning walker striding along the coast path at Heybrook bay.

Evening light on the orange cliffs at Goodrington Sands.

Brixham's' old harbour at last light.